# MASTERING

## THE CRAFT OF

# COPYWRITING

*Techniques and Strategies*
*for Success*

## Michael H. Finck

*Michael H. Finck*

## Dedication

To all the writers, marketers, and storytellers who are passionate about the power of words. May this book be a guide and inspiration on your journey to master the craft of copywriting and connect with your audience in meaningful ways. Dedicated to those who never stop learning, growing, and striving for success.

# Foreword

Copywriting is an art and a science. It requires both creativity and strategy to craft words that engage, inform, and persuade. And in today's fast-paced, digital world, the importance of effective copywriting has never been greater. Whether you're a marketer, advertiser, or business owner, the ability to write compelling copy that connects with your audience is a critical skill.

This book, "*Mastering the Craft of Copywriting*", is a comprehensive guide for anyone looking to master the art of copywriting. Written by a seasoned copywriter, it provides practical techniques and strategies for writing copy that drives results. From understanding your audience to tracking your success, this book covers it all.

Whether you're a seasoned copywriter or just starting out, this book is a must-read. It's a valuable resource that will help you hone your craft, grow your skills, and achieve success in your writing and marketing efforts. So, dive in and start mastering the art of copywriting today.

# Table of Contents

# Introduction

In "*Mastering the Craft of Copywriting*", you will learn the skills and strategies needed to become a successful copywriter.

Copywriting is the art of crafting persuasive messages that inspire and motivate your audience to take action. It's a crucial skill for anyone looking to succeed in marketing, advertising, or sales. Whether you're a seasoned professional or just starting out, this book will provide you with the tools and techniques you need to create compelling copy that converts.

Throughout the book, we'll cover a wide range of topics, including:

- The fundamentals of copywriting, including how to write headlines that grab attention, craft compelling body copy, and create powerful calls to action

- Techniques for crafting persuasive messages, such as using storytelling, emotional appeals, and social proof

- Tips and tricks for writing copy that converts, including how to write for different audiences, test and optimize your copy, and measure the effectiveness of your campaigns

- Insights and strategies from some of the world's top copywriters, including best practices and real-world examples

Whether you're a seasoned professional or just starting out, "Mastering the Craft of Copywriting" will provide you with the tools and techniques you need to succeed as a copywriter.

By the end of this book, you'll have a solid foundation in the principles and practices of copywriting, as well as the skills and confidence to create effective, persuasive copy for any situation. So let's get started!

# Chapter 1

## Introduction to Copywriting: The Basics

In this chapter, I'll cover the fundamentals of copywriting and give you an overview of what you'll learn in this book.

So, what exactly is copywriting?

Simply put, it's the art of crafting persuasive messages that inspire and motivate your audience to take action. Whether you're writing an email, a landing page, or a social media post, the right words can make all the difference in getting your message across and driving results.

Copywriting is a crucial skill for anyone looking to succeed in marketing, advertising, or sales. It's about understanding your audience, grabbing their attention, and persuading them to take the desired action.

It requires creativity, strategy, and the ability to craft compelling messages that connect with your audience emotionally.

In the subsequent chapters of this book, I'll delve into the fundamental principles of copywriting and advanced techniques and strategies that will help you create compelling, effective copy. I'll cover topics such as:

- How to write compelling headlines that grab attention and set the stage for your message

- Techniques for crafting persuasive body copy, including the use of storytelling, emotional appeals, and social proof

- Tips for writing copy that converts, including how to write for different audiences, test and optimize your copy, and measure the effectiveness of your campaigns

- Insights and strategies from some of the world's top copywriters, including best practices and real-world examples

By the end of this book, you'll have a solid foundation in the principles and practices of copywriting and the skills and confidence to create compelling, persuasive copy for any situation.

# Headlines: The First Impression

Your headline is often the first thing your audience will see in copywriting. It's your chance to grab their attention, establish your credibility, and set the stage for your message. In this section, I'll delve into the art of crafting compelling headlines that get your message across and inspire your audience to keep reading.

First, let's start with the basics. A *headline* is a brief statement or question that summarizes your message and captures the essence of your offer. Copywriting is designed to entice your audience and persuade them to take the next step, whether that's clicking on a link, signing up for a newsletter, or making a purchase.

To craft a compelling headline, you need to understand your audience and what they're looking for. What problem are they trying to solve? What benefits are they seeking? By answering these questions, you can create a headline that resonates with your audience and motivates them to take action.

Here are a few tips for crafting compelling headlines:

- Keep it brief and to the point. Aim for around 6-8 words, depending on the length of your message.

- Use strong, actionable words that inspire your audience to take action. Words like *"discover," "unlock,"* and *"transform"* are great choices.

- Make it clear and specific. Avoid vague or general statements that don't give your audience a clear idea of what to expect.

- Test different versions of your headline to see which performs best. You can use tools like Google Analytics or A/B testing to see which headline gets the most clicks or conversions.

In addition to crafting compelling headlines, you should also be aware of common pitfalls to avoid. Here are a few things to watch out for:

- Avoid using clickbait headlines that overpromise and under-deliver. Your audience will quickly lose your trust if you don't deliver on your promises.

- Don't use jargon or technical language that your audience may not understand. Please keep it simple and easy to understand.

- Don't use sensationalist or controversial headlines just for attention, as this can backfire and damage your reputation.

By following these tips and avoiding common pitfalls, you'll be well on your way to crafting compelling headlines that grab your audience's attention and set the stage for your message.

Copywriting is essential because it is the face of your brand. It is the first point of contact between your business and your target audience and sets the tone for future interactions. A well-crafted message can make a lasting impression on your target audience and help build trust and credibility for your brand.

It's essential to understand that copywriting is not just about writing; it's about understanding your target audience and crafting a message that speaks to them directly. Copywriting requires careful research, planning, and execution.

A copywriter must be able to communicate complex ideas clearly and concisely, using language and tone that resonates with the target audience.

In conclusion, copywriting is a critical component of modern marketing, and businesses of all sizes and industries need to invest in mastering the craft of copywriting.

In the following chapters, we will delve deeper into the various techniques and strategies for success in copywriting, including researching your target audience, crafting compelling headlines, writing persuasive body copy, and much more.

# Chapter 2

## Crafting Persuasive Body Copy

Now that you've grabbed your audience's attention with a compelling headline, it's time to delve into the body of your message. In this chapter, we'll cover the essential techniques for crafting persuasive body copy that keeps your audience engaged and motivates them to take action.

## Audience

First and foremost, it's essential to understand your audience and what they're looking for. What are their pain points? What are their goals? You can tailor your message to address their needs and interests by answering these questions.

## Structure and Language

Next, you'll want to structure your body copy in a way that's easy to read and understand. The structure means using short paragraphs, bullet points, and subheadings to break up your text and make it more digestible.

It would be best if you also used simple, straightforward language that's easy to understand, even for people unfamiliar with your topic.

In addition to structure and language, you'll also want to use persuasive techniques to engage your audience and motivate them to take action. Some standard techniques include:

- **Storytelling:**

Use anecdotes and examples to illustrate your points and make your message more relatable and engaging.

- **Emotional appeals:**

Use emotions to connect with your audience and persuade them to take action. Emotional appeals can include using fear, guilt, or hope to motivate your audience.

- **Social proof:**

Use testimonials, case studies, and other social proofs to show your audience that others have successfully used your product or service and achieved positive results.

By using these persuasive techniques and structuring your body copy in a clear and easy-to-read way, you'll be well on crafting a compelling body copy that engages your audience and motivates them to take action.

In addition to these tips, you should also be aware of common pitfalls to avoid. Here are a few things to watch out for:

- Don't use jargon or technical language that your audience may not understand. Please keep it simple and easy to understand.

- Use simple sentence structures and avoid using long, rambling paragraphs. Keep your sentences short and to the point.

- Don't use filler words or fluff to pad your copy. Stick to the essentials and get to the point quickly.

By following these tips and avoiding common pitfalls, you'll be well on your way to crafting persuasive body copy that engages your audience and motivates them to take action.

# Calls to Action: Closing the Deal

Now that you've grabbed your audience's attention with a compelling headline and engaged them with persuasive body copy, it's time to close the deal with a powerful call to action. This section will cover the essential techniques for crafting calls to action that convert and drive results.

A call to action (CTA) is a statement or button that prompts your audience to take a specific action, such as signing up for a newsletter, making a purchase, or downloading a whitepaper.

It's a crucial element of any copywriting campaign, as it's the point where you ask your audience to take the next step and move closer to becoming a customer.

To craft a compelling CTA, you'll want to keep a few things in mind:

- ***Make it clear and specific:***

Your CTA should be clear and specific, telling your audience exactly what you want them to do. Avoid vague or general statements that don't give your audience a clear idea of what to expect.

- ***Use strong, actionable language:***

Use words that inspire your audience to take action, such as "*sign up*," "*download*," or "*buy now.*"

- ***Use a sense of urgency:***

Encourage your audience to act now using language that suggests a limited-time offer or a sense of urgency. Words like "*hurry,*" "*limited* time," or "*don't miss out*" can be effective in motivating your audience to take action.

## Common Pitfalls to Avoid

In addition to these tips, you should also be aware of common pitfalls to avoid. Here are a few things to watch out for:

- Don't use aggressive or pushy language that comes across as spammy or salesy. Aggressive or pushy language can turn off your audience and damage your reputation.

- Don't use multiple CTAs within the same message. Multiple CTAs (Call To Action) can confuse your audience and dilute the effectiveness of your message.

- Don't use CTAs that are not relevant to your audience. Make sure your CTA aligns with your audience's interests and needs.

By following these tips and avoiding common pitfalls, you'll be well on your way to crafting powerful calls to action that drive results and convert your audience into customers.

# The Power of Words: Understanding How Language and Tone Impact the Effectiveness of Copy

In copywriting, words are more than just letters on a page - they are the building blocks of your message and can make or break your campaign. Understanding the power of language and tone is crucial for creating compelling copy that resonates with your target audience and drives results.

## Language

Language is the foundation of communication, and choosing the right words to convey your message is essential. The right words can evoke emotions, build trust, and motivate action. On the other hand, the wrong words can confuse, mislead, and turn off your target audience. Copywriters must carefully consider their words and how the target audience will perceive them.

## Tone

The tone is also a critical factor in effective copywriting. The styling and tone refer to the attitude or mood conveyed by the words in a message. Different styles can evoke diverse emotions in the reader, and choosing the right tone that aligns with your message and resonates with your target audience is essential.

For example, *a playful, lighthearted tone might be appropriate for a social media post promoting a new product. In contrast, a serious, professional tone might be more suitable for a business-to-business marketing campaign.*

Incorporating the right language and tone into your copywriting can be challenging, but it's essential for success. It requires a deep understanding of your target audience and their needs and the ability to craft a message that speaks to them directly.

Here are a few tips to help you incorporate effective language and tone into your copywriting:

### 1. *Know your target audience:*

Tailor the language and tone you use to your target audience and their preferences.

### 2. *Keep it simple:*

Use clear, concise language that is easy to understand. Avoid using technical terms or industry jargon that might confuse or alienate your target audience.

### 3. Be consistent:

Consistency is fundamental in copywriting, and it's essential to maintain the same tone and language throughout your message.

### 4. Experiment:

Feel free to experiment with different tones and language styles to find what resonates best with your target audience.

In conclusion, understanding the power of words and how language and tone impact the effectiveness of copy is crucial for creating compelling messages that resonate with your target audience and drive results.

In the next chapter, we will explore the importance of research and writing for different audiences.

# Chapter 3

# Writing for Different Audiences

As a copywriter, it's essential to understand that not all audiences are created equal. Different people have different needs, interests, and motivations, hence; you should tailor your copy to address these differences.

In this chapter, we'll cover the essential techniques for writing copy that speaks to different audiences and motivates them to take action.

First, let's start with the basics.

Before you start writing, you must understand your target audience and what they're looking for. Ask yourself these questions:

- Who are they?

- What are their pain points?

- What are their goals?

You can tailor your message to address their needs and interests by answering these questions.

Next, you'll want to consider the tone and style of your copy. Different audiences may respond better to different tones and styles, so choosing the right one for your message is vital.

*For example, a younger, more casual audience may respond better to a conversational tone, while a more formal audience may prefer a more serious, professional manner.*

In addition to tone and style, you'll also want to consider the language and terminology you use.

Different audiences may have different levels of familiarity with your topic, so it's vital to use language that's appropriate and easy to understand.

Suppose you're writing for a technical audience. In that case, you may use more technical language and jargon, while if you're writing for a general audience, you'll want to use simpler, more straightforward language.

By following these tips and tailoring your message to your target audience, you'll be well on crafting copy that speaks to different audiences and motivates them to take action.

In addition to these tips, you should also be aware of common pitfalls to avoid. Here are a few things to watch out for:

- Don't assume that all audiences are the same. Different people have different needs and interests, so it's important to tailor your message accordingly.

- Don't use language or terminology that your audience may not understand. Keep it simple and easy to understand.

- Don't use the same tone and style for every audience. Different audiences may respond better to different tones and styles, so it's imperative to choose the right one for your message.

By following these tips and avoiding common pitfalls, you'll be well on your way to crafting copy that speaks to different audiences and motivates them to take action.

## Storytelling in Copywriting

Storytelling is a potent weapon in the field of copywriting. It allows you to connect with your audience on an emotional level and persuade them to take action. This section will cover the essential techniques for using storytelling in your copy to engage and motivate your audience.

First, let's start with the basics. What is storytelling in copywriting?

Simply put, it's the art of using anecdotes, examples, and narratives to illustrate your points and make your message more relatable and engaging. By using storytelling, you can bring your message to life and make it more memorable and effective.

So, how do you use storytelling in your copy? Here are a few important tips to get you started:

- *Use anecdotes and examples to illustrate your points:*

Anecdotes and examples are great ways to bring your message to life and make it more relatable. Using real-world examples, you can show your audience how your product or service has helped others and how it can help them.

- **Use a narrative structure:**

A narrative structure is a way of organizing your story clearly and logically. A narrative structure can include using a beginning, middle, and end and characters and plot points to illustrate your points.

- **Use emotions to connect with your audience:**

Emotions are a powerful tool in storytelling. Using emotions to communicate with your audience, you can create an emotional connection that motivates them to take action.

By following these tips and using storytelling in your copy, you'll be well on your way to engaging and motivating your audience. In addition to these tips, you should also be aware of common pitfalls to avoid. Here are a few things you must avoid when crafting you copy:

- Keep it simple and relatable, and don't use overly complicated or unrealistic stories.

- Don't use storytelling just for the sake of storytelling. Ensure your story serves a purpose and ties back to your message.

- Don't use storytelling to manipulate or deceive your audience. Manipulating or deceiving your audience can damage your reputation and credibility.

By following these tips and avoiding common pitfalls, you'll be well on your way to using storytelling in your copy to engage and motivate your audience.

## Research and Planning: The Key to Effective Copywriting

Before you start writing, it's essential to have a plan in place. Research and planning are critical components of effective copywriting and can help ensure that your message resonates with your target audience and drives results.

Research is the first step in every copywriting process. To research involves learning as much as possible about your target audience, including their needs, preferences, and pain points.

This information will help you craft a message that speaks directly to your target audience and motivates them to take action.

To conduct effective research, consider using a variety of methods, including:

### 1. Surveys:

Ask your target audience about their needs, preferences, and pain points through online surveys or focus groups.

### 2. Demographic research:

Use data from sources such as the census or market research firms to understand the demographic characteristics of your target audience.

### 3. Competitor research:

Study the messages and strategies used by your competitors to understand what works and what doesn't.

Once you have completed your research, it's time to start planning your copywriting campaign. This campaign involves outlining the key messages you want to convey, determining the tone and language you will use, and creating a structure for your message.

A well-structured message will be straightforward for your target audience to follow and understand, and it will help you stay on track as you write.

When planning your copywriting campaign, consider the following:

### 1. Objectives:

Objectives simply mean what you want the reader to do after going through your copy. What do you want to achieve with your copywriting campaign? What actions should your target audience take?

### 2. Key messages:

What are the essential points you want to convey to your target audience?

### 3. Tone and language:

How do you want your message to come across to your target audience?

### 4. Structure:

How will you organize your message to make it easy for your target audience to understand and follow?

In conclusion, research and planning are crucial components of effective copywriting. By taking the time to research your target audience and plan your campaign, you can create a message that resonates with your target audience and drives results.

In the next chapter, we will explore using emotional appeals to craft compelling headlines that grab attention and motivate action.

# **Chapter 4**

# Using Emotional Appeals in Copywriting

Emotional appeals are a powerful tool in the world of copywriting. They allow you to connect with your audience on an emotional level and persuade them to take action. This chapter will cover the essential techniques for using emotional appeals in your copy to engage and motivate your audience.

First, let's start with the basics. What are emotional appeals? Simply put, they are techniques that use emotions to persuade your audience to take action. Emotional appeals can include using fear, guilt, hope, or other emotions to connect with your audience and motivate them to take action.

So, how do you use emotional appeals in your copy? Here are a few tips to get you started:

- ***Identify your audience's emotional triggers:***

Different people have different emotional triggers, so it's essential to identify what motivates your audience. What are they afraid of? What do they hope for? You can tailor your message to address their emotional needs and motivations by answering these questions.

- ***Use strong, actionable language:***

Use words that inspire your audience to take action, such as *"protect," "prevent,"* or *"achieve."*

- *Use storytelling to illustrate your points:*

Storytelling is a powerful tool for creating emotional connections with your audience. By using anecdotes, examples, and narratives, you can bring your message to life and make it more relatable and engaging.

- *Use images and visuals to enhance your message:*

Visuals can be a powerful tool for creating emotional connections with your audience. By using images and graphics that illustrate your points and evoke emotions, you can enhance your message and make it more impactful.

- *Test different emotional appeals to see which ones work best:*

Different emotional appeals may work better for different audiences and situations, so it's crucial to test different approaches to see what works best. You can use tools like A/B testing or surveys to measure the effectiveness of your emotional appeals.

## Common Pitfalls to Avoid When Using Emotional Appeals

In addition to these tips, you should also be aware of common pitfalls to avoid. Here are a few things to watch out for:

1. Don't use emotional appeals just for the sake of emotion. Ensure your message is relevant and tied to your audience's needs and interests.

2. Don't use emotional appeals to manipulate or deceive your audience. Using emotional appeals that manipulate or deceive your prospects can damage your reputation and credibility.

3. Don't use emotional appeals to exclude logic and reason. Using emotional appeals

and logical arguments to create a well-rounded, persuasive message would be best.

4. Don't overdo it: While emotional appeals can be effective, it's crucial to do it sparingly. Too much emotion can come across as artificial or manipulative, which can turn off your audience.

5. Don't use inappropriate or offensive emotions. Some emotions, such as fear or guilt, can be powerful motivators, but they can also be inappropriate or offensive if misused. It's imperative to use these emotions judiciously and with sensitivity to your audience's needs and feelings.

6. Don't use the same emotional appeal for every audience. Different audiences may respond better to separate emotional appeals, so it's vital to tailor your message to your audience's needs and interests.

By following these tips and avoiding common pitfalls, you'll be well on your way to using emotional appeals in your copy to engage and motivate your audience.

## Crafting Compelling Headlines: How to Grab Attention and Drive Results

The headline is the first thing your target audience sees, and it can make or break your copywriting campaign. A well-crafted headline will grab attention, pique interest, and motivate action.

On the other hand, your prospective audience will overlook a weak headline, and your message will never be seen.

So, how do you craft compelling headlines that drive results? Here are some tips to help you get started:

### 1. *Be concise:*

Your headline should be short, sweet, and to the point. Avoid using complex language or long, drawn-out sentences.

### 2. *Make it relevant:*

Your headline should be relevant to your target audience and their needs. Use the research you conducted in Chapter 3 to ensure your headline speaks directly to their pain points and interests.

### 3. *Create a sense of urgency:*

Use words and phrases like "*now*," "*today* ", and" *limited time only*" to create a sense of urgency and motivate your target audience to take action.

### 4. *Ask a question:*

Asking a question in your headline can effectively grab attention and engage your target audience.

### 5. Use strong, active verbs:

Use strong, active verbs in your headline to create a sense of excitement and encourage action.

### 6. Make it unique:

Your headline should stand out from the crowd and be unique to your brand and message.

In addition to these tips, it's essential to test your headlines to see what works best. Try different headlines with different segments of your target audience to see which resonates most.

In conclusion, crafting compelling headlines is a crucial step in copywriting. Following these tips can create headlines that attract attention, pique interest, and motivate action. In the next chapter, we will explore the best practices when writing for the web.

# Chapter 5

# Writing for the Web: Best Practices

The world of copywriting is rapidly changing, and with the rise of the internet, it's more important than ever to know how to write effectively for the web. This chapter will cover the essential best practices for writing for the web, including tips for creating compelling headlines, structuring your content, and using visuals and multimedia to enhance your message.

First, let's start with the basics. What makes web copy different from other forms of copywriting? Here are a few crucial factors to consider:

- **Attention span:**

People tend to have shorter attention spans when reading online, so it's essential to get to the point quickly and keep your message concise and easy to understand.

- **Scannability:**

People often scan web pages rather than reading every word, so it's important to use formatting techniques like headings, bullet points, and bolding to make your content more scannable and easy to understand.

- **Links and multimedia:**

The web is a rich multimedia platform, so it's important to use links and multimedia elements like videos, images, and audio to enhance your message and keep your audience engaged.

So, how do you write compelling web copy?

Here are a few fundamental tips to get you started with writing compelling copies:

- **Use compelling headlines:**

Your headline is often the first thing your audience will see, so it's important to make it attention-grabbing and relevant to your message.

- **Use short paragraphs and bullet points:**

Short paragraphs and bullet points are easier to read and understand than long, rambling blocks of text.

- **Use links wisely:**

Links can be a powerful tool for providing additional information and resources to your audience, but it's important to use them wisely. Don't overuse links or use irrelevant or spammy links, as this can damage your credibility and reputation.

- **Use formatting and design elements to enhance your message:**

Formatting elements like headings, bolding, and italics can make your content more understandable. Design elements like color, typography, and layout can also enhance your message and make it more visually appealing.

- **Use online and other social media platforms to promote your content:**

Social media and other online platforms can be powerful tools for promoting your content and reaching a wider audience. Use these platforms wisely and consistently to build your brand and engage with your audience.

## Common Pitfalls to Avoid When Writing For the Web

In addition to these tips, you should also be aware of common pitfalls to avoid when writing for the web. Here are a few critical determining factors to watch out for:

- Don't use jargon or technical language that your audience may not understand. Keep it simple and easy to understand.

- Don't use overly complicated sentence structures or long, rambling paragraphs. Ensure the sentences in your copy are precise and to the point.

- Don't use filler words or fluff to pad your copy. Ensure to always stick to the essentials and get to the point quickly.

By following these tips and avoiding common pitfalls, you'll be well on your way to writing effective web copy that engages and motivates your audience.

# Understanding Your Target Audience: Writing Copy that Resonates

To write copy that resonates with your target audience, you must deeply understand their needs, preferences, and pain points. The more you know about your target audience, the better equipped you'll be to write copy that speaks directly to them and motivates them to take action.

Here are essential tips for understanding your target audience and writing copy that resonates:

### 1. *Know their pain points:*

What are the challenges and problems that your target audience is facing? Understanding their pain points will help you write copy that speaks directly to their needs and offers a solution.

### 2. Identify their motivators:

What motivates your target audience to take action? Understanding their motivators will help you write copy that appeals to their wants and desires.

### 3. Use their language:

Use the language and terminology that your target audience is familiar with. Using their language will help you connect deeper and build trust with them on a larger scale.

### 4. Know their preferences:

When writing copies, you need to know the preferences of your target audience. For example, *know what kind of messages they respond to best or what sort of tone they prefer (formal or conversational)*. Understanding their preferences will help you write copy that speaks directly to them.

### 5. Anticipate objections:

What objections might your target audience have about your product or service? Anticipating these objections will help you write copy that addresses their concerns and motivates them to take action.

By following these tips, you'll be able to write copy that speaks directly to your target audience and resonates with them. These tips, in turn, will help you drive results and achieve your copywriting objectives.

In conclusion, understanding your target audience is crucial to effective copywriting. By getting to know your target audience and writing copy that resonates with them, you'll be able to create a message that motivates them to take action.

# Writing Persuasive Body Copy: Strategies for Engagement, Information, and Conversion

The body of your copy is where you delve deeper into the details of your message and offer solutions to your target audience's pain points and challenges. Writing persuasive body copy is an art that requires a combination of storytelling, persuasion, and a deep understanding of your target audience.

Here are some strategies for writing persuasive body copy that engages, informs, and convinces your audience:

### 1. *Tell a story:*

People are naturally drawn to stories, and using storytelling techniques in your body copy can help you engage your audience and build emotional connections.

## 2. *Use clear, concise language:*

Keep your language simple, straightforward, and easy to understand. Avoid using technical jargon or complex terms that your target audience might not be familiar with.

## 3. *Highlight benefits:*

Focus on the benefits of your product or service rather than just the features. Explain how it will solve your target audience's pain points and make their lives easier.

## 4. *Address objections:*

Anticipate your target audience's objections about your product or service and address them directly in your body copy. Addressing objectives will help you build trust and overcome any objections holding them back from taking action.

### 5. Use imagery:

Use images and visual aids to help illustrate your message and make it more engaging.

### 6. Make it actionable:

Encourage your target audience to take action by including CTAs (calls to action) throughout your body copy.

### 7. Emphasize urgency:

Use language that creates a sense of urgency and motivates your target audience to take action.

By following these strategies, you'll be able to write body copy that engages, informs, and convinces your target audience. Your body copy should build trust and motivate action, so be sure to focus on your product's or service's benefits and include calls to action that encourage action.

In conclusion, writing persuasive body copy is essential to effective copywriting. By focusing on engagement, information, and conversion, you'll be able to create a message that resonates with your target audience and motivates them to take action.

# Chapter 6

## The Power of Social Proof in Copywriting

Social proof is a powerful tool in the world of copywriting. It refers to the idea that people are more likely to take action if they see others doing the same thing. In this chapter, we'll explore the concept of social proof and how you can use it effectively in copywriting to engage and motivate your audience.

*First, let's start with the basics. What is social proof?*

Simply put, it's the idea that people are more likely to take action if they see others doing the same thing. Social proof can be particularly effective in marketing and advertising, as it can help build trust and credibility with your audience.

So, how do you use social proof in your copywriting? Here are a few tips to get you started:

- ***Use testimonials and reviews:***

Testimonials and reviews from satisfied customers can be a powerful form of social proof. You can build trust and credibility with your audience by sharing real-world examples of how your product or service has helped others.

- ***Use numbers and statistics:***

Numbers and statistics can be powerful social proof, providing concrete evidence that your product or service is adequate. For example, having a high customer satisfaction rate or a large number of users can help build trust and credibility with your audience.

- *Use influencer endorsements:*

Influencer endorsements can be a powerful form of social proof, as they can help give your product or service credibility and reach a wider audience. By partnering with influencers in your industry, you can leverage their audience and credibility to promote your product or service.

By following these tips and using social proof in your copywriting, you'll be well on your way to engaging and motivating your audience.

## Common Pitfalls to Avoid When Using Social Proof

In addition to these tips, you should also be aware of common pitfalls to avoid when using social proof. Here are a few things to watch out for:

- Don't use fake or fabricated testimonials or reviews. Fabricated reviews or testimonials can damage your reputation and credibility.

- Don't use outdated or irrelevant testimonials or reviews. Use current and relevant examples to build trust and credibility with your audience.

- Don't rely solely on social proof. While it can be a powerful tool, using it with other persuasive techniques is vital to create a well-rounded, compelling message.

By following these tips and avoiding common pitfalls, you'll be well on your way to using the power of social proof in your copywriting to engage and motivate your audience.

# The Art of Persuasion: Techniques and Strategies

Persuasion is a crucial skill in the world of copywriting. It drives your audience to take action and makes your message compelling. This section will cover the essential techniques and strategies for persuasion in copywriting.

First, let's start with the basics. What is persuasion in copywriting? Simply put, it's the art of using words and techniques to motivate your audience to take action. Persuasion can include emotional appeals, storytelling, social proof, and other methods to engage and inspire your audience.

So, how do you persuade your audience in your copywriting? Here are a few tips to get you started:

- **Use emotional appeals:**

Emotional appeals are a powerful tool for connecting with your audience and persuading them to take action. Using emotions like fear, guilt, hope, or happiness, you can create an emotional connection with your audience and motivate them to take action.

- **Use storytelling:**

Storytelling is a powerful tool for persuading your audience. By using anecdotes, examples, and narratives, you can bring your message to life and make it more relatable and engaging.

- **Use social proof:**

Social proof is the idea that people are more likely to take action if they see others doing the same thing. Using testimonials, reviews, and influencer endorsements, you can build trust and credibility with your audience and persuade them to take action.

By following these tips and using persuasion techniques in your copywriting, you'll be well on your way to engaging and motivating your audience.

## Pitfalls to Avoid When Persuading Your Audience

In addition to these tips, you should also be aware of common pitfalls to avoid when persuading your audience. Here are a few things to watch out for:

- Don't manipulate or deceive your audience, as these antics can damage your reputation and credibility.

- Don't rely solely on one persuasion technique. Use a variety of techniques to create a well-rounded, persuasive message.

- Don't overdo it. Too much persuasion can come across as pushy or manipulative, which can turn off your audience.

By following these tips and avoiding common pitfalls, you'll be well on your way to using the art of persuasion in your copywriting to engage and motivate your audience.

# Using Storytelling Techniques to Create an Emotional Connection with Your Audience

Storytelling is essential to copywriting and can be a powerful tool for creating an emotional connection with your target audience and driving conversions. By using storytelling techniques, you can create a narrative that connects with your target audience on a deeper level and helps to build trust and credibility.

Here are some tips for using storytelling in your copywriting:

### 1. Start with a story:

Start your copy by introducing a relevant story to your target audience. Use the story to set the stage and provide context for the rest of your message.

### 2. Use vivid details:

When telling your story, use vivid details that help to paint a picture in your target audience's mind. Vivid information will help to make the story more memorable and engaging.

### 3. Highlight the emotional journey:

Focus on your protagonist's emotional journey and how they overcome obstacles to achieve their goal. Highlighting the emotional journey will help to create an emotional connection with your target audience and make your message more impactful.

### 4. Make it relatable:

Your story should be relatable to your target audience. Use language and scenarios that they can easily identify with and connect to.

### 5. Tie it back to your message:

At the end of your story, tie it back to your message. Explain how the story relates to your product or service and why it's relevant to your target audience.

### 6. Keep it simple:

When using storytelling in your copywriting, ensure to keep it simple and focused. Avoid convoluted stories that are difficult for your target audience to follow.

### 7. *Practice and refine:*

Practice and refinement are vital to using storytelling effectively, and both are important, just like with any other aspect of copywriting. Keep practicing and refining your storytelling skills until you find a style that works best for your target audience.

In conclusion, storytelling is a powerful tool for creating an emotional connection with your target audience and driving conversions. By using vivid details, highlighting the emotional journey, and keeping it simple and relatable, you'll be able to create stories that resonate with your target audience and drive results.

# Chapter 7

## Testing and Optimizing Your Copy

Testing and optimizing your copy is an essential step in the copywriting process. It allows you to see what works and what doesn't and make adjustments to improve the effectiveness of your message. In this chapter, we'll explore the concept of testing and optimizing your copy and how you can use this process to create more compelling copy.

First, let's start with the basics. Why is testing and optimizing your copy important? Simply put, it allows you to see what works and what doesn't and make adjustments to improve the effectiveness of your message. Testing and optimizing your copy can be crucial in marketing and advertising, where the stakes are high, and every word counts.

So, how do you test and optimize your copy? Here are a few tips to get you started:

- **Use A/B testing:**

A/B testing is a simple but effective way to compare two versions of your copy and see which one performs better. By testing different headlines, calls to action, or other elements of your copy, you can see what works and doesn't and make adjustments accordingly.

- **Use analytics tools:**

There are a variety of analytics tools available that can help you track and analyze your copy's performance. These tools can provide valuable insights into how your audience interacts with your copy and what changes you can make to improve its effectiveness.

- ***Get feedback from your audience:***

Getting feedback from your audience to see how they are responding to your copy is essential. Doing this include using surveys, focus groups, or other methods to gather feedback and see what's working and what's not.

By following these tips and using testing and optimization techniques, you'll be well on your way to creating more effective copy that engages and motivates your audience.

## Common Pitfalls to Avoid When Testing and Optimizing Your Copy

In addition to these tips, you should also be aware of common pitfalls to avoid when testing and optimizing your copy. Here are a few pitfalls you should avoid when testing and optimizing your copy:

- *Don't make too many changes at once.*

It can be tempting to make many changes all at once, but knowing what's working and what's not can make it challenging. Instead, make small changes one at a time and track their results to see what works best.

- *Don't rely solely on data.*

While data is essential, it's also important to consider other factors, such as your audience's needs and preferences and the overall goals of your campaign.

- *Don't get too caught up in testing and optimization.*

It's crucial to find a balance and stay calm in the process. Make adjustments as needed, but trust your instincts and be willing to take risks.

By following these tips and avoiding common pitfalls, you'll be well on your way to testing and optimizing your copy to create more effective messages that engage and motivate your audience.

## Measuring the Effectiveness of Your Copywriting

Measuring the effectiveness of your copywriting is an essential step in the copywriting process. It allows you to see how well your copy performs and make adjustments to improve its effectiveness.

In this section, we'll explore the concept of measuring the effectiveness of your copywriting and how you can use this process to create more compelling copy.

First, let's start with the basics. Why is measuring the effectiveness of your copywriting important? Simply put, it allows you to see how well your copy performs and make adjustments to improve its effectiveness.

Measuring the effectiveness of your copy can be particularly important in marketing and advertising, where the stakes are high, and every word counts.

So, how do you measure the effectiveness of your copywriting? Here are a few tips to get you started:

- *Use analytics tools:*

There are a variety of analytics tools available that can help you track and analyze your copy's performance. These tools can provide valuable insights into how your audience interacts with your copy and what changes you can make to improve its effectiveness.

- **Use A/B testing:**

A/B testing is a simple but effective way to compare two versions of your copy and see which one performs better. By testing different headlines, calls to action, or other elements of your copy, you can see what works and doesn't and make adjustments accordingly.

- **Use metrics:**

There are a variety of metrics you can use to measure the effectiveness of your copy, such as conversion rate, click-through rate, and engagement rate. Tracking these metrics allows you to see how well your copy performs and make adjustments as needed.

By following these tips and using measurement techniques, you'll be well on your way to creating more effective copy that engages and motivates your audience.

In addition to these tips, you should also be aware of common pitfalls to avoid when measuring the effectiveness of your copy. Here are crucial pitfalls you should watch out for when measuring the effectiveness of your copy:

- Don't rely solely on one metric. It's essential to consider a variety of metrics to get a complete picture of your copy's performance.

- Don't make changes based on short-term results. Tracking your copy's performance over time is essential to get a more accurate picture of its effectiveness.

- Don't get too caught up in measurement. It's crucial to find a balance and not get too bogged down in the process. Make adjustments as needed, but trust your instincts and be willing to take risks.

## Tips for Measuring the Effectiveness of Your Copywriting

Here are some additional tips for measuring the effectiveness of your copywriting:

- ***Use customer feedback:***

In addition to tracking metrics, getting feedback from your customers to see how they respond to your copy is essential. This can include using surveys, focus groups, or other methods to gather feedback and see what's working and what's not.

- ***Use qualitative data:***

In addition to tracking quantitative metrics like conversion rate, it's also vital to consider qualitative data like customer comments and feedback. Qualitative data can provide valuable insights into how your audience perceives your copy and what changes you can make to improve its effectiveness.

- **Use heat maps and scroll maps:**

Heat maps and scroll maps can provide valuable insights into how your audience interacts with your copy. These tools can show you where people are clicking and what they are reading, which can help you see what's working and what's not.

By following these tips and using various measurement techniques, you'll be well on your way to creating more effective copy that engages and motivates your audience.

It's essential to keep in mind that measuring the effectiveness of your copywriting is an ongoing process. It's not something you do once and forget about but rather a continuous process of testing, measuring, and adjusting to optimize your copy's effectiveness.

# Optimizing for Search Engines and Incorporating SEO Best Practices into Your Copywriting

In today's digital age, having an online presence is critical for businesses of all sizes. But with so many websites competing for the exact keywords, it can take time to get noticed by your target audience and this is where SEO comes in handy.

By incorporating SEO best practices into your copywriting, you can improve your website's visibility and drive more traffic.

Here are some tips for optimizing your copywriting for search engines:

### 1. *Research keywords:*

Begin by researching relevant keywords that are closely related to your target audience and business. Use tools like Google Keyword

Planner to find popular keywords with high search volume.

## 2. Use keywords strategically:

Incorporate keywords into your copywriting naturally and strategically. Don't over stuff the keyword, as this can negatively impact your website's ranking.

## 3. Create valuable and informative content:

Search engines typically favor websites that provide informative and valuable content to their users. Ensure your website's high-quality content offers value to your target audience.

## 4. Optimize for readability:

Make sure your copywriting is easy to read and understand. Use clear, concise language and break up your content into smaller, more manageable chunks.

### 5. Use header tags:

Use header tags to structure your content and make it easier for search engines to understand the hierarchy of your content.

### 6. Incorporate internal links:

Permanently Link to other pages on your website using internal links. Incorporating internal links helps search engines understand the structure of your site and can improve your website's ranking.

### 7. Use descriptive and meaningful URLs:

Use descriptive and meaningful URLs that accurately reflect the content on your page.

Using descriptive and meaningful URLs can improve your website's click-through rate and ranking.

### 8. Monitor your website's performance:

Regularly monitor your website's performance using tools like Google Analytics. Monitoring your website's performance will help you identify areas for improvement and track your progress over time.

In conclusion, optimizing your copywriting for search engines is critical for improving your website's visibility and driving more traffic to your site.

By incorporating SEO best practices into your copywriting, you'll be able to create a user-friendly and search engine-friendly website, helping you reach and engage your target audience more effectively.

# Chapter 8

## Advanced Copywriting Techniques

Advanced copywriting techniques are a set of strategies and tactics that experienced copywriters use to craft more compelling and persuasive messages.

In this chapter, we'll explore some of the most common advanced copywriting techniques and how you can use them to create compelling copy.

## Using Storytelling

One advanced copywriting technique is the use of storytelling. Storytelling is a powerful tool for engaging and persuading your audience. By using anecdotes, examples, and narratives, you can bring your message to life and make it more relatable and engaging.

## Using Emotional Appeals

Another advanced copywriting technique is the use of emotional appeals. Emotional appeals are a powerful tool for connecting with your audience and persuading them to take action. Using emotions like fear, guilt, hope, or happiness, you can create an emotional connection with your audience and motivate them to take action.

## Using Advanced Copywriting Techniques

A third advanced copywriting technique is the use of scarcity. Scarcity refers to the idea that people value things more when they are rare or in limited supply. By using *scarcity* in your copy, you can create a sense of urgency and motivate your audience to take action.

Other advanced copywriting techniques include:

- **Social Proof**: The use of social proof is the idea that people are more likely to take action if they see others doing the same thing.

- **Power Words**: The use of power words is words that trigger strong emotional responses.

- **Cliffhangers**: The use of cliffhangers is techniques that leave your audience wanting more and create a sense of suspense.

Using these advanced copywriting techniques, you can craft more compelling copy that engages and motivates your audience. It's important to remember; however, to ensure to use these techniques sparingly and appropriately, as overuse can come across as manipulative or pushy.

By using these techniques wisely and in combination with other persuasive techniques, you'll be well on your way to creating copy that resonates with your audience and drives results.

## Insights from Top Copywriters: Best Practices and Real-World Examples

Insights from top copywriters can be a valuable resource for anyone looking to improve their copywriting skills and create more compelling and persuasive messages. This section will explore best practices and real-world examples from top copywriters that can help you create compelling copy.

## Understanding Your Audience

One critical insight from top copywriters is the importance of understanding your audience. Before you start writing, it's essential to spend time researching and understanding your target audience and what motivates them.

Understanding your audience can include identifying their needs, pain points, and goals and using this information to craft a message that resonates with them.

## Simplicity and Clarity

Another fundamental insight from top copywriters is the importance of simplicity and clarity. The best copy is clear, concise, and easy to understand. It gets to the point quickly and avoids jargon or technical language that may confuse your audience.

## Using Persuasive Techniques

A third crucial insight from top copywriters is the importance of using various persuasive techniques. The best copy uses storytelling, emotional appeals, and social proof to engage and persuade the audience. Using multiple strategies, you can create a more well-rounded and persuasive message.

## Testing and Optimizing

Other insights from top copywriters include the importance of testing and optimizing your copy and measuring its effectiveness. By testing and measuring your copy, you can see what works and doesn't and make adjustments to improve its effectiveness.

By following these best practices and real-world examples from top copywriters, you'll be well on your way to creating compelling copy that engages and motivates your audience.

## Measuring Success: Techniques for Tracking and Analyzing the Performance of Your Copywriting

As a copywriter, it's essential to track and analyze your work performance to determine what's working and what's not. By measuring the success of your copywriting, you can make data-driven decisions that will improve your results and help you reach your goals.

Here are some techniques for measuring the success of your copywriting:

### 1. Set goals and KPIs:

Start by setting clear and measurable goals for your copywriting. Determine the key performance indicators (KPIs) that will help you track your progress towards these goals.

### 2. Use tracking tools:

Use tracking tools like Google Analytics to track your website's performance and copywriting. Tracking tools will help you understand how your audience interacts with your content and identify areas for improvement.

### 3. Analyze website traffic:

Analyze the number of visitors to your website and the sources of that traffic. Determine which channels are driving the most traffic to your site and focus on optimizing those channels.

### 4. Track conversions:

Track the number of conversions your copywriting is generating. Determine which pages on your site are driving the most conversions and optimize those pages for better performance.

### 5. Monitor engagement metrics:

Monitor metrics like time on site, bounce rate, and page views to understand how engaged your audience is with your content.

### 6. Analyze social media metrics:

If you're using social media to promote your copywriting, track metrics like engagement, reach, and clicks to determine the success of your efforts.

### 7. Conduct surveys and focus groups:

Conduct surveys and focus groups to get feedback from your target audience. Conducting surveys and focus groups will help you understand how your audience perceives your copywriting and identify areas for improvement.

### 8. Continuously monitor and refine your approach:

Regularly monitor the performance of your copywriting and make data-driven decisions to improve results. Continuously refine your approach based on your findings to ensure that you continually improve and achieve your goals.

In conclusion, measuring the success of your copywriting is essential for improving your results and reaching your goals. By tracking and analyzing the performance of your work, you'll be able to make data-driven decisions that will help you achieve your objectives and create copywriting that genuinely resonates with your target audience.

# Conclusion

In conclusion, "Mastering the Craft of Copywriting" is a comprehensive guide to the art and science of copywriting. In this book, we've explored a variety of topics related to copywriting, including the basics of copywriting, advanced techniques, best practices from top copywriters, and strategies for persuasion, testing and optimization, and measuring effectiveness.

Throughout the book, we've provided tips, examples, and case studies to help you understand the concepts and apply them in your own work. By following the strategies and techniques outlined in this book, you'll be well on your way to mastering the craft of copywriting and creating powerful and effective copy that engages and motivates your audience.

To put it all together, here are a few key takeaways from this book:

- Understanding your audience is key to effective copywriting. By researching and understanding your target audience's needs, pain points, and goals, you can craft a message that resonates with them and motivates them to take action.

- Simplicity and clarity are essential in copywriting. The best copy is clear, concise, and easy to understand. It gets to the point quickly and avoids jargon or technical language that may be confusing to your audience.

- A variety of persuasive techniques can be used to engage and persuade your audience. These can include storytelling, emotional appeals, social proof, and other techniques that connect with your audience on an emotional level.

- Testing and optimizing your copy, and measuring its effectiveness, are important steps in the copywriting process. By tracking metrics and gathering feedback, you can see what works and what doesn't, and make adjustments to improve the effectiveness of your message.

By following these key takeaways and continuing to learn and improve your copywriting skills, you'll be well on your way to mastering the craft of copywriting and creating powerful and effective copy that engages and motivates your audience.

# Epilogue

As you reach the end of this book, you should now have a solid foundation in the craft of copywriting. You've learned about the various techniques and strategies for writing engaging, informative, and persuasive copy that resonates with your target audience.

By applying the concepts and techniques outlined in this book, you'll be able to create copywriting that engages, informs, and convinces your audience. Whether you're writing for a website, a blog, a social media platform, or a traditional advertising medium, you'll have the tools and knowledge you need to succeed.

However, mastering the craft of copywriting is a journey, not a destination. There's always room for improvement and new techniques to learn. As you continue to hone your skills and gain experience, you'll find new ways to engage and connect with your target audience.

So, keep practicing and never stop learning. With dedication and perseverance, you'll be able to create copywriting that truly stands out and helps you achieve your goals.

We hope this book has been a valuable resource for you and that it has helped you on your journey towards mastering the craft of copywriting.

Good luck and happy writing!

# About the Author

Michael H. Finck is a seasoned copywriter and marketing expert with over 9 years of experience in the industry. Michael has worked with a wide range of clients, from small startups to large multinational corporations, helping them to craft compelling copy that connects with their audience and drives results.

Michael H. Finck has a passion for writing and a talent for storytelling, and has been recognized for [their achievements and awards]. *"Mastering the Craft of Copywriting"* is Michael's first book, drawing upon his wealth of experience and expertise in the field of copywriting to provide practical techniques and strategies for success.

Michael H. Finck is excited to share his knowledge with others and help them to achieve success in their copywriting and marketing efforts.

# THE END